21 Steps to Guarantee your Dream Job Anywhere in Canada

A Step by Step Success Manual for New Canadian Immigrants: Job Market Inside Tips, Techniques & Tricks. Get Ahead of Everyone Today !

by Ian Khan PMP, B.E., MCSE

21 Things that Guarantee your Dream Job Anywhere in Canada - A Step by Step Success Manual for New Immigrants

by Ian Khan

Books may be purchased by contacting the publisher and author at www.iankhan.com

Cover Design: Marketicious Inc
Interior Design: Marketicious Inc
ASIN No ISBN: B00RHAG9K6
BUSINESS & ECONOMICS > Careers > Job Hunting
SELF-HELP > Personal Growth > Success
First Edition

Published on Amazon

Author Bio

Ian Khan is a multifaceted first generation Canadian based in Toronto Canada. He is one of the thousands of people who have migrated to Canada and search for a better career, better life and freedom of living and just like many of you has gone through the struggles of setting down in Canada, calling it home and succeeding !

As a first generation immigrant, the experience gained by one is tremendous in helping everyone else who follows. As one who has seen it and done it, being able to facilitate the journey of others is key in being able to contribute to the social fabric. Experiences referred to in this book are first hand experiences and based on what the author has personally seen and experienced. In his career today, Ian is responsible for managing large teams of individuals, hiring new team members and as such selecting candidates, conducting interviews and shortlisting resumes. The ideas and steps mentioned in this book are what the author uses most of the times and what recommends as best practices. These are also techniques that have been used by studying hundreds of books and journals by the author throughout his career spanning over 15 countries. In essence this is the condensed nectar that you need in order to get ahead when looking for a job in Canada and a starting point to understand the job search process and what it entails.

Ian is heavily involved in the technology circles in promoting Cloud Computing, SaaS and other technology platforms. He frequently speak speaks at events, technology conferences and is a well sough after speaker and technology and business professional. He is also the author of a number of books, also available on Amazon, that are included on the next page.

Other Titles by the Author

Get Ahead - 30 Home Based Businesses to Start in 2015:
Learn what is new, what is hot, and what makes money !

Sell to Me: *The Enterprise Software Marketing Survival Guide*

21 Steps to Guarantee your Dream Job Anywhere in Canada
- A Step by Step Success Manual for New Canadian Immigrants

Make Me Like You: *The Essential Guide to Getting Your Resume Noticed by the Toughest Hiring Managers*

How I Used an Easy Way to Stop Smoking Forever: *Get Rid of the Frustration of Quitting and Easily Succeed without any Remorse*

Cloud Wars: *Learn what is driving growth on the Cloud and why the Big Guys like Microsoft, Google and Amazon have already declared War on each other.*

"Dedicated to the thousands of brave souls, who choose to build new lives in new lands every day!"

A Something Extra Special for my Readers !

As a token of my appreciation towards my dedicated readers, I am excited to offer a pre-launch insider access to my upcoming books.

Join my mailing list to be the first one to know about my book releases, special offers and a chance to win one of my books for free.

Signup at www.iankhan.com/newsletter

It's FREE, Fast & Easy to Sign Up!

Introduction

Every new immigrant in Canada arrives with dreams, hopes and a goal of creating a better life. Immigration itself is a major task to accomplish and after the years of waiting, the stress and jumping multiple hoops, every immigrant dreams of integrating with the Canadian society and becoming a part of the fabric that millions of people from all over the world have embraced. Well life is not in the early years. After landing in Canada you are faced with the daunting task of looking for a pace to stay, getting your papers in order and then applying for jobs in the local market. This is where the going gets tough for most people.

Getting a good paying, satisfying job in Canada is like any other developed country. Companies need qualified workers, you have a resume, you think you fit the bill, and you apply. After a few weeks you may get a call for an interview and maybe even get the job, or get turned down. For those that get the jobs, things may seem better, but more often than once, you may have to apply for a new job and a new position. Sometime sit may take weeks or even months to find the right fit.

In this book you will learn from the experiences of real landed immigrants in Canada, their job search experiences, and their career choices, you will lean more than just how to apply for a job. You will learn how to get in front of the hiring manager and to show them why you are the best candidate for the position. In addition, learn about the various industries, seasons for hiring and the insider view of hiring in any industry. Learn from the authors experiences of looking for jobs, getting interviews and landing successful jobs in the Canadian market.

If you are a landed immigrant in Canada or are going to become one shortly, this book is a must read to be successful in your job search right when you land and be fully prepared even before you set foot on Canadian soil !

Set yourself apart from the thousands of immigrants who land in Canada every year and take lead in your job search and be successful.

Let us get started! We have a lot to do.

Ian Khan
January 2015, Toronto

Contents

Step 1

Find Out Who You Truly Are

They say that charity begins at home and as such the first thing to do before embarking on this massive endeavour of finding the next best career opportunity that suits you is to take stock off your situation. This is the opportunity for you to find out for yourself the things that you're good at and things that you're not good at the things. This may also include stuff you like to do and those that you don't. It's very important to know who you really are. Being in the wrong job is by far worse than being in a lower paying job of your choice. The toll that something that you don't like plays is not easy do deal with. You may be tempted to jump into a job at the job search stage but trust me it is essential to have your job aligned with your values, priorities and overall life situation.

Although a job search is pressing short term need, the effect on the long term is substantial. It is essential to maintain an utmost priority of being able to find work in the line of your preferences. For this very reason it is essential to find out what you need in life, in your career and so on. If you have already undergone this process then you are way ahead in the game.

There are many resources available to do this. There are literally hundreds of books available that can help you learn and navigate the waters of finding yourself. Really, you have to do the hard work beforehand and not after you've ended up with what you think is the idea job. Speakers like Brian Tracy, Anthony Robbins, Deepak Chopra and many more have written countless books that really talk about finding your calling, finding your goals, and finding you. I strongly recommend that you look at a

few of these books and read them cover to cover and find out
what is it that drives you and what values you bring to the table
that could really help you sell. Some of my recommendations are,

Antony Robbins
- Unlimited Power
- Awaken the Giant

Dale Carnegie
- How to Win Friends and Influence People

Norman Vincent Peale
- The Power of Positive Thinking

Napoleon Hill
- Think and Grow Rich

Jack Canfield
- The Success Principles
- The Power of Focus
- The Aladdin Factor
- Dare to Win

These are not just books but amazing tools to build your character
and personality in many ways, including a career.

When you arrive in Canada you will encounter a number of
different industries, different types of people from all kinds of
races, religions, and nation's. Everybody has the same goals, i.e
to succeed in life and to provide the best for their families and
themselves as part of this community of people.

Let's make sure that you start off with the right foot and that your
steps towards integrating in the Canadian social fabric are done
in a way that works best for you. Remember, the people around
you are the people that you will be working tomorrow in some
capacity or the other. As such it becomes essential that you really
understand how the Canadian Society works. A majority of
Canadians for example love hockey. A number of us again love

the snow, and we can go on and on with a huge list of what Canadian like. One of the best ways to really integrate into Canada is to make friends. Make friends with your neighbors make friends with the people at the gas station, and really everyone you meet. Once you start getting into the habit of making friends, trust me, people will reciprocate your goodwill and help you every day for the rest of your life.

Use this as the fundamental building block of your integration in Canada.

Step 2

Get A Feel For The Local Market

Now that you have found out who you are what your interests are and where you belong in terms of your career, it is important to know the local market. Getting to know industries are hiring , knowing what drives the revenues of your province, what drives the city you live will be important in helping target your next job opportunity.

Canada is a very large country with 8 provinces. Based on the province, the dominant industry may be different or they may have one or more businesses that the province is strong in. As an example Quebec is very focused on creating goods that are made of wood forestry lumber and so on its focus is on wood based industries. The Prairie Provinces are more focused on agriculture, and in the west Alberta is focused on oil sands. If you have a background in engineering or oil or energy you might be the well-off looking for job opportunities in Alberta. So, start looking around and find out what drives your region. It's also important to speak to the right people such as employment agencies, and get a feel for what sectors are hot in hiring. A good resource to get information is the Government of Canada website. Here are some Canadian Government websites to get started. Some of the sites are non-job related, but are good examples of showcasing an overall Canadian Government website.

Find a Job
Employment Insurance
Canada Revenue Agency
Canada Pension Plan retirement pension

You can also visit job boards and Internet job sites to get a feel for what sector is hiring in your city. In this book that will also learn later on how to customize your resume and to make it very focused on the job that are targeting. It is essential to get an understanding of sectors that are hot, jobs that are in demand, and what is happening in your city and region overall. Career fairs, job shows, mas hiring and many other things could be all happening at the same time. You need to be connected to the grid to know it all.

Let's get started go ahead and check some local the sites newspaper as industry magazines and even your local library to see what industries are heavily hiring in your city. Let's also find the top employment agencies that are active within your community and city.

Step 3

Build Your Hit List

Whether you like it or not, you have to be super organised to get anything done. Planning out and executing a plan are two essentials to do anything in life, let alone the act of searching for a job, which has a pretty high priority. Let get started with one of the most essential things that lay down the foundation of your job search success.

In Step 3, we will build a list of potential companies that you would like to for. Really let's get real. Do not think that you possess the skills or experience, at this stage it's purely the fact that I believe I would love to work for these companies attitude. You can use a paper and pen, a notepad or a computer to keep all your efforts in one place. My recommendation is to work off a computer/laptop/tablet device to keep everything in one place, however you may choose to get organized the way you organize the best.

Target a list of anywhere between 25-100 companies that you would like to work for. These can be identified based on the industry, your experience and so on. These have to be realistic options where you could find the position you are looking for. These could be companies that are similar to your previous workplace, if you have worked before. As an example, if you are experienced in retail sector this would potentially include targeting large chains such as Walmart, Sears, the Bay and so on. If you are from a technology background then looking at tech companies would be the right step.

Lets get the list going. Start working on the list right now and before you go ahead any further. This is Step 3 and needs to be completed before you move on any further.

Step 4

Applying to Open Job Positions

Applying to jobs in Canada can be done using various means. Here is a quick run though of what works in the Canadian Job market and when to use each method.

Personally Handed Resumes

Although this is a bit hard to do purely because of the time consuming effort this takes, you may end up giving you resume to people that ask for it. This would be known associates, friends and so on. On a local level if you end up applying to firms that operate locally, or that have specifically asked for Resumes to be handed in person, this would work as a good option. For smaller stores and operations that employ less people this sometimes works best. We will talk about resume formatting and what to include in your resume in later steps. That will help.

Public Job Boards

Some of the popular job boards in Canada are Workopolis, Monster, Job Shark and other small ones. Workopolis is the most popular of them all and boasts hundreds of new job listings every day. Most of the job board openings are usually paid for the company that is posting the jobs, so job openings are genuine. One disadvantage that you may face on the larger boards is that you may not be able to personally connect with the hiring manager, or create a personalised cover letter, both of which are important for the overall job search process. Nevertheless, you will have to create customised resumes no matter where you apply or what method you use.

Company Job Boards

Many times you will have t apply t jobs through the company job boards. These are the recruitment platforms that companies want candidates to apply though. One of the popular ones is Taleo, which a number of organizations have as the default candidate management system. For every organization you will have to create a login and password and also create a comprehensive candidate profile. This is a time consuming task, but needs to be done unfortunately.

Email
Sending resumes by email is very common in Canada. Email is very common for organizations that are medium to large sized, although for the larger companies, the job boards are mostly the preferred medium of receiving resumes. Its is usually harder to identify who the hiring manager is and to know other insider tipis about the position. Over email you are most likely to submit a cover letter and your resume. In terms of formats, Microsoft Word or PDF formats work very well, the latter being my recommendation as it retains all the formatting.

As a to-do let's create job seeker accounts on a few popular websites such as Workopolis.com and Monster.ca. This will be a good start. You can also start working on creating a profile on LinkedIn.com, if you have not done so yet. We will talk about LinkedIn in detail on our Step 12, which is dedicated to using the power of social networks to apply for jobs.

Step 5

Build a Compelling Base Resume

The ever elusive resume. Some say creating a great resume is an art, some say it's the achievements that really make it shine through. No matter who says what, the resume is one of the most important pieces of the puzzle in getting the right job.

-       What is the format of a resume?
-       What should i include?
-       What should I omit from my resume?

and so many more questions.

You will find countless books and resources on how to build a resume that gets you the job. Well in this book we are not going to reinvent the wheel. We will however talk about some key resources in building a great resume and what works in the Canadian job market.

Here are some aspects of a resume you need to maintain.

Keep your resume clear, crisp, and concise.
Do not include any Photographs
Do not include personal details such as date of birth, passport number, marital status etc,
Keep your resume only to professional accomplishments, roles and duties.

You will most likely be ok with a one to two page resume in 99% of your job applications. In case you have exceptional experience and need to have a resume on more than 2 pages, be wary of making it too lengthy and consider attaching your work as a portfolio instead.

It's time to head to the library. Yes, you don't expect everything to be handed to you on a silver spoon. We have to make haste, test a lot of waters and do a lot of exciting things. So let's get your resume in order. No matter if you choose a chronologic ort a functional resume, make it full of impact. Some highly recommended resources are below.

Guerrilla Marketing for Job Hunters

What Color Is Your Parachute? 2015: A Practical Manual for Job-Hunters and Career-Changers

Knock 'em Dead Resumes: A Killer Resume Gets More Job Interviews!

A good way to know if your resume is good enough is to show it to a friend or even head down to the local community center and speak to a councillor.

Step 6

Where To Find Job Openings

There are literally hundreds of places to look for a job. Here are some of the common places you may find them.

Online Job sites.

- Local community newspapers
- Local Ethnic Newspapers (European, Asian, all communities in Canada have multiple publications)
- Local city newspapers (Every City has one or more of these usually)
- Kijiji.ca
- Craigslist.ca
- Simplyhired.ca
- Indeed.ca
- Linkedin.com
- www.workopolis.com

In addition to these you can also look at Government of Canada websites.

Government of Canada Job Bank

Step 7

How To Target Unlisted Jobs

They say that the unlisted job market has more than 80% of job openings. This market is never advertised but it exists. How do we end up unlocking this market? The answer lies in going above and beyond just looking for jobs on the job boards, websites and company portals. This is a game above the ordinary, but here is the good news. You can use this channel to find out if there are opportunities that exist for you, target those opportunities and land up with a good career opportunity ! It happens all the time., but only to people who know how to make it work to their advantage.

Start building your network of associates within the industries you work in or would like to work in. This could include attending local networking events, conferences, meet up groups, professional associations and so on. You could be having a conversation at the local community center where there is an unadvertised opening or even with a friend who knows a certain someone who is hiring. Personal connections are key to making this happen things this way.

Other ways to reach out to prospective employers is by building connections over professional networks such as LinkedIn and other job related social media platforms. We'll talk about social media and job search options in upcoming Steps.

Getting involved in the community and in professional circles can help a lot in your career. This not only at the time of looking for a job but also to build connections that will sometimes last over a lifetime. Look for professional organizations and associations in your city town or region that you can be a member of, and get to know people who are in the same profession as yours. If you are unable to find any professional organizations that relate to your profession then get involved in community causes. Canada is a very active community of people and in every city and town you will find numerous causes that people support and help regularly. Getting to know people and acquaint yourself with them is a great way to build long lasting friendships and professional connections. People also engage with the community through regular monthly events, weekly outings and other such initiatives that help their groups do the work that they believe in. I encourage you to visit websites such as www.meetup.com and finding what kind of groups exist in your neighbourhood and city

Grab a pen and paper and start building a list of all the community centers, agencies, and professional associations, neighborhood associations within your city region or province. Then get in touch with them over e-mail phone and find out what it takes to be a member. Start building your network in person and over the Internet by engaging in dialogs with people on social network websites that we will see in upcoming chapter.

One of the techniques to get your foot into the door is also to send unsolicited resumes to your potential employers. This may not work as a strategy for large employers because you will be blocked off by systems such as job boards and career portals that large organizations typically use. Unless you know the hiring manager directly or you have a list of people who run the organization or the department where you are applying it could be a huge waste of time. Instead you might as well focus your efforts on small and medium size companies find out the decision makers contact details and send them you resumes with a great cover letter, which we will find how to do in our next steps. Although a good option to use when you're applying for a generic position, it may not work well in your benefit because customizing you resume is important in applying for every job. So although I do believe this option exists to apply for jobs, it is not my best recommendation to do so. But again it depends on what job you are applying to and the nature of the position.

Here are some resources to get started.

www.meetup.com
www.kijiji.ca
www.craigslist.com
http://goo.gl/E99Nu2 (This is a very long list of all associations across Canada. Thanks to the Government of Canada)

Step 8

Optimize Your Resume

As I mentioned in my previous steps you resume is perhaps one of the most important pieces off the puzzle that will help you plan to create job. Having said that the resume is more than just your experiences your work profile and everything else your employer needs to know about. The objective of having a resume is not to be seen, but to be read in full and then used as a reason to call the candidate for an interview. Really, that's all and that's what a resume is supposed to do.
Again, a resume is supposed to get you an interview!

I must require when applying for any job is to be able to match your resume to the position responsibilities and the role that has been hired for. Every job opportunity that you apply for you will have to customize your resume and cater it to the requirements of the position. Now keep in mind the job opportunity actually has to be something in line with your overall experience and skill set.

Every time you apply for a job identify the key words that are being used in the position to describe the roles and responsibilities qualifications and qualities of the ideal candidate. Matching the keywords from a job description two your resume is key in creating a customized can resume. To understand by me do this keep in mind that many recruitment websites and hiring platforms now employ automatic technologies weed out resumes that are not keyword heavy pertaining to the position they are hiring for. Mind you and we're not seeking any information that are really doing more often is SEO for the resume. It therefore becomes important to be able to first of all recognize the keywords that should be used in your resume if you are applying for a specific position. Second is using these keywords in your resume so that all the information is cohesive and flows.

Remember if you get called for an interview you should be able to vouch for these things you claim you have done in your resume.

Please and undermine the importance of using this technique to make you resume pass the automatic test. It takes a lot of effort and energy to apply for every job in the last thing you want to do is for your resume to be weeded out by some computer program that does not know how qualified or skilled you are.

You will need to do this for every job that you apply to. No excuses!

Step 9

The Cover Letter Has It All

The cover letter is very important. A majority of the candidates often neglect the importance of sending a well-crafted cover letter along with the resume. The cover letter provides the hiring manager an insight into what values you bring to the organization and other aspects of your experiences you would like to highlight for the position that you have applied to.

Remember a cover letter has to be short, crisp, and concise and relate to relevant information to the hiring manager with respect to your unique aspects and strengths and how they relate to the position. As a result of this, the cover letter you submit for every job needs to be customized to that particular job and position. Yes absolutely it's a lot of work but then who said looking for jobs was easy. There are thousands of qualified job aspirants applying for every job every single day. Canada is a very talented country and also the talent pool within Canada because of highly skilled and qualified immigrants is very high. It is not surprising to find a hundred or a few hundred applicants for a single job application. Trust me, I speak this from experience of hiring for key positions and receiving flood of resumes that never stop coming in. How do you want to stand out from the rest of the crowd? Getting a job offer is a far off thing. We first need to be able to conquer is to get and succeed at interviews.

Back to the cover letter please do not underestimate the power of a well-crafted cover letter. If possible get a professional writer to write a cover letter for you or you can simply create a letter on their own just remember making open and honest and accurate.

There are hundreds of books available in book stores that will help you create a cover letter. Not all hiring managers will ask for a cover letter every time, however I strongly suggest that you submit one with every job application that you send this will make you stand out from the crowd and increase the chances of being called for the interview had been shortlisted faster.

Some of the key aspects to remember renewal are getting your cover letter together are:

- Keep your cover letter one page or 3/4 page long
- Do not exceed more than 300 to 415 words on your cover letter
- Address the cover letter to the right person of if you have been able to find out the hiring managers contact details.
- Make sure there are no spelling or dramatic and mistakes in the cover letter or the resume
- Proofread your cover letter at least twice before you actually sending out
- You can send the cover letter in word format or PDF of format (same as Resume)
- Use generic fonts and font sizes that will work of the size and the font sizes for Headings.
- Put your contact details at the bottom of the cover letter

When you're done crafting your cover letter, read and think if you were the hiring manager would you hire the person who has written to cover letter? That's your greatest litmus test to put s stamp of approval on your nicely done cover letter. Don't move to the next Step unless you have written the Cover letter.

Step 10

Spend Time on Communication

Canada being a bilingual country, with English & French as official languages makes it necessary for everyone to be able to speak at least one of these languages fluently. Communication is key in getting ahead in every aspect in Canada and if you are weak in communication, it may not work very well in your favor. You may find it harder to get interviews, or even follow ups after your phone interviews and conversations. It is just very important to be able to keep communication clear and to be good at your speaking skills. Try to spend as much time as possible in learning English, both spoken and written to your best abilities. You have to give this a very high importance overall as this directly affects your ability to not only just get a job, but to get a position that is beyond the ordinary. Research has proved that the earning ability of professionals is directly related to their ability to communicate and if you don't have good English or French skills you are at a disadvantage.

Based on where you reside, you may not need to learn both English and French, In Quebec, French is heavily used and very little English is spoken. So if you are in Quebec you already know the importance of learning French. For the rest fo Canada you will be ok if you learn English only. People around Canada overall do not speak a lot of French or should I say are more conversant in English. Here are some tips to get better on your language skills

- Join a local language speaking group

- Meet people at a local community center or a learning center. You will find a lot of free classes being offered

- Watch videos on YouTube or loo for a language learning resource online

- Spend a lot of time listening to native speakers and try to emulate their pronunciations

- Increase your vocabulary by learning a few words every day.

- Don't be shy in speaking to people in English or French. If you don't speak you will not learn.

Step 11

The Inner Game

Job hunting is in itself a full time job. You probably must have heard this hundreds of times. This statement is absolutely true and clearly signifies the importance of taking your job search seriously. Unless you are committed 100 percent every single day unless and create a schedule for yourself where your activities are planned clearly identifying prospective employers to target, and resumes to send out ,your job search is going to be mediocre and as a result will yield mediocre results.

Don't be surprised if you do not get called for interviews or your resume does not have the traction that you desire. Hunting for jobs in a tough market like Canada is not easy but with some tricks tips and the right approach you could be on your way to having a great career opportunity and a well-paying job. Perhaps the biggest issue or force that opposes a good job search is the mind. If you have bad financial situation or are under stress your job search needs to be unaffected by these influences. It is also very important to keep clear focus and not let your job search get disrupted by other things happening in your life. In this case you need to be able to separate your priorities from your emotions.

Always find a quiet place to work out of and even go to a public library to spend time. You will often find that many others like you will be at libraries referencing books, magazines and meeting with other job seeker. The point is to focus and avoid distractions and focus. Jon hunting is also about being proactive and not reactive to job postings. In one of our steps I mentioned targeting the unlisted job market which is a reality and which will need a hundred percent commitment. Canada has hundreds and thousands of qualified immigrants, people who are PhD's and hold master's degrees in their countries, and hence a huge pool of candidates. It's not surprising to see people with a qualifications barely surviving in low paying jobs or working for minimum wage jobs. We all have seen it and yes it is painful to see that qualified people in places that they do not deserve, but maximizing your potential is of prime importance. You need to be able to turn every rock and every leaf in order to get the position and the career opportunities that you desire.

I have seen people struggle for a long time and then succeed like nothing before. Maintain the highest level of priority and urgency when it comes to looking for a job and finding that position.

Step 12

Make Social Networks Work

Social media can be very helpful when looking for work. In the Canadian job market social media although not used for resume submissions, social media is often used by hiring companies to promote their job postings. Candidates can benefit from being active on social media and learning about what new positions are being posted.

Social media can also be a hindrance, if you have inappropriate things posted on your social media streams. It's very common for employers to look at your profile and see what kind of social media activity you are engaged in.

Make sure that you have the right privacy controls enabled and that your profile reflects the professional personality you would like to portray. Of course depending on what job position you are applying for and what company you are applying to, employers may or may not check your social media profiles. It is better however to have a clean slate and put your best foot forward. I have heard of candidates being rejected after passing numerous stages but failing because of inappropriate or contradictory posts o-r photos made on social media. I also use social media to check a candidates profile when I am hiring. I use it as a tool to see if the candidate is what they say they are. I also commonly Google the names of the candidate and see what search results come up. It just helps put together a complete picture and profile of the candidate from a hiring managers perspective.

Get your social media profile up to date. Also enable and play around with your social media settings as needed to enable or disable aspects of your profile as needed. This is a key Step.

Some common social media networks include

www.linkedin.com
www.facebook.com
www.twitter.com
www.pinterest.com
www.youtube.com
http://goo.gl/kGcxZh (Long list of Social Media Networks)

Step 13

LinkedIn Mastery

LinkedIn is one of the most popular social media platforms for professional development. LinkedIn boasts millions of users worldwide whose only goal is to develop their networks professionally

LinkedIn is a great option to look for jobs. The LinkedIn jobs section has a very active list of jobs. On an everyday basis are posted by employers that are desperately seeking candidates. LinkedIn being a professional platform offers the convenience of having a qualified pool of candidates to choose from. This works very well with employers. In fact when I am hiring for any positions within my team, I extensively use LinkedIn to seek the right candidate. I'm a big fan of LinkedIn and I have used the platform extensively to build my networks over the years. I also use it to communicate with my friends, networks, colleagues and to create engagement. My recommendation for you is to create a very strong LinkedIn profile that you will not only be able to use to your job search but also to build your professional networks join professional groups and build an overall career growth that's not only focused on the job search. There are some really great books available that talk about how to optimize your LinkedIn profile with do's and don'ts of using LinkedIn successfully. At a very high level here are my recommendations that are a must for every professional whether you are looking for a job or not.

- Create a LinkedIn profile that is 100% complete
- Do not skip any sections that you think you can complete
- Make your LinkedIn profile and accurate and precise with dates
- Include all your professional designations certificates degrees and educational credentials

- Use a good professional picture in your LinkedIn profile if

After you are done, you can use your LinkedIn profile to apply for jobs. I would highly recommend that you should also and always accompany your LinkedIn job applications with a copy of your PDF formatted resume. Once you apply for a job on LinkedIn your profile is automatically attached to the job application that is sent to the employer and it will work really well in your favor if you have a well-crafted LinkedIn profiled along with a nicely done resume. Remember everything works in conjunction with everything else and you have to make sure that all aspects of your professional presence are clean and crisp and as powerful as possible.

With these steps you should be able to use LinkedIn in a much better fashion than before. Let's get started and get a stellar LinkedIn profile created. Do not move to the next Step unless you have a profile on LinkedIn that you are proud of !

Step 14

Passing The Personality Tests

Quite often you will be subjected to one or more personality tests as part of your screening and interview process. These can get daunting but most of the times stick to the Myer Briggs tests or suchlike. There are also specific platforms that offer personality testing as part of their screening process. Websites such as Clearfit have developed comprehensive personality profiles that they use to provide services to employers.

Here are some tips to get through the personality tests and excel at the results.

- Always be truthful about your answers and never fake your answers.
- Take your time when answering your questions, but be mindful of anytime time limitations
- Always find a suitable time and place to do the personality tests.
- Distractions can be a major hurdle and you will need your full attention when doping these tests.
- Sometimes No answer is right or wrong, so don't try to skew your answers to be of a specific personality type.

Take some free personality tests online as part of your preparation towards getting a new job

Here are some tests to get you started.

http://www.humanmetrics.com
http://www.16personalities.com

Did you take any personality tests? What did you find from the results? You can now move to the next step.

Step 15

Excel at the Phone Interview

Phone interviews are usually a sign that the prospective employer is interested in you. If you have a phone interview with a recruiter they probably just want to gauge you and see how you communicate and answer questions and discuss any specifics in your profile. Keep in mind that although phone interviews are great, they are tricky as the person on the other side can only hear your voice and are unable to see your whole personality. That challenge makes phone interviews tricky. Here are some things to keep in mind when having a phone interview.

- Always pick a quiet non disturbing place to have the phone interview
- Be comfortable and ready for the call at least 5 minutes before the actual time.
- Keep a pen and paper handy to take any notes during the interview
- Take the 5 minutes to put your thoughts together and to quickly recap the opportunity and what you bring to the table
- During the call, listen carefully and give the other person the time to complete their sentences
- Take your time when providing answers and speak in a clear concise way
- Note down all aspects of the discussion that you find interesting in your notes
- Towards the end of the interview always make sure to ask if there was any additional information the interviewer needs

- Always remember to ask about what the next steps in the hiring process are
- Send a Thank you note by email, thanking the interviewer for the opportunity to speak with them over the phone.

Step 16

Icing on The Cake : The Thank You Note

Make sure that you send a thank you email to your interviewer after the interview. This has to be done within the next 12 hours of your interview. The note can be as simple as thanking the interviewers for their time and hoping to hear from them soon. Sending the thank you note is essential and key in making a great impression with the interviewers.

Here is a sample of a very short thank you note that you can send to your interviewer after the interview.

Dear John

I wanted to thank you for your time yesterday and helping me understand where your organization is going in terms of growth and expansion. As discussed I possess a very strong skill set that can help empower your organization into growth and success as per your vision. I'm very keen in knowing the next steps in the interview process as I am very excited in this opportunity.

Kind Regards
Ian Khan

A Thank you note can be as simple as this. The important part is that you must send a thank you note. This makes a great impression on the interviewers and increases your chances of being further shortlisted and called for the next round of interviews.

It's ok to send a thank you note as an email if you managed to get if from the person who met you during the interview. You can also mail the Thank you note if you do not have the persona email but have their mailing address.

Bottom Line – Send a Thank you note every time you have an interview!

Step 17

Job Search Etiquette

- The entire process of searching for a suitable job and finally landing up with the opportunity can be a lengthy process. Here are some essentials to keep in mind while maintaining the etiquette of job hunting.

- Respect everyone you come across in this process

- Respect other job seekers and never ever belittle anyone

- Be mindful of other people's time

- Always address people correctly

- Always speak and write your best English

- Never send communication with spelling mistakes.

- Give people time to respond back to you

- Never overcall or over email when following up.

- Maintain a window of at least a day when expecting to hear back from people

- Be polite and respectful in every email or letter you send out

- Feel free to ask for time to respond if you need to.

- Never leave people hanging for an answer when they are expecting reply

- Aways meet your timelines and deadlines

- Do not expect leeway or personal favours by strangers

- Push for results in a diplomatic manner so as not to hurt anyone's sentiments or personality

- Never make personal comments about anyone

- Always keep people informed if you are running late

- Always inform anyone expecting reply if you are going to be late in respond

- Always keep people informed if you are not going to be available and they would want to know

- Do not call people over the weekend and expect a reply

- Bes respectful of peoples private time and family

- Always give people more than one option of being able to contact you if possible

- Enable voicemail on your phone if possible and record a clear, concise professional greeting

Step 18

Questions to ask your Interviewer

An interview is a two way street. As much as your prospective empowers is trying to know about you, feel free to ask your prospective employers any questions you may have. Feel free to ask your interviewer questions regarding the position, the role, responsibilities, major tasks and what kind of the day you can expect at the workplace. It's important that you have a clear understanding of the job and the responsibilities associated. For some job profile such as in sales it's important to ask for sales quotas and things that that determined your overall success. I also highly recommend you to ask the interviewer how you will be measured in the job in terms of success. It's important to get this cleared up at the beginning and during the process of the interviews. This also tells the employer that you are looking at the job from more than a money perspective, Remember for employers, money is just one aspect. They are trying to look for a person who would rightly succeed in the jab profile and not just stayed there for the sake of getting a paycheck. Asking the right questions during the interview can really speed up your own candidacy in the job process. Feel free to ask the HR person about things like vacation time, hours of work, resources that you will have available, scheduled holidays and so on.

If you are in a multi interview situation with more than one person that includes say a senior level manager or a hiring manager and the HR person, it's always great to address the person related and ask them to question pertaining to the role within the hiring process. In this case I wouldn't ask the CEO about the timings of work and the days of work, instead you should direct these questions to the HR. The CEOs focus is about growing the organization, it's about bringing a vision together, increasing revenues, increasing or improving customer services and so on. Make your questions relevant to the person and the role. Don't waste anyone's time during the interview.

Believe it t not, asking questions during an interview is a great thing. Everyone understand that the candidate may have questions. Here are some of the questions you can ask without any hesitations.

- What is the overall compensation of the position?
- How will my performance be evaluated?
- How often will my performance be evaluated
- Who will I be reporting to?
- Do I have anyone reporting to me?
- What are the working hours?
- What is the dress code?
- What is your policy on bringing kids to work?
- What is your policy on bringing pets to work?
- What is your policy on flex hours?
- What is your policy on working from home?

These are just some of the things you can ask during the interview. Of course keep in mind that you will have to gauge the status of your overall interview success in order to be confident to ask any of these questions. Also try not to ask any questions that do not pertain to your profile or that do not affect you in any way.

Step 19

Questions Interviewers Cannot Ask You

Yes, there are questions that an employer's cannot ask a candidate during the interview. If the questions affect the candidates overall suitability towards the job, these questions cannot be asked. And also if the questions have nothing to do with the job responsibilities and skills of the candidate they are not to be asked. That's it!. Some of the highly taboo questions are;

- Questions regarding age
- Questions regarding marital status
- Questions regarding sexual orientation
- Questions regarding family and plans to have children
- Questions regarding pregnancy and if you're planning to get pregnant
- Questions regarding your ethnic background
- Questions regarding you're a race
- Questions regarding your political affiliations
- Questions regarding your religious views

This is just a brief list. But yes, employers cannot ask you questions regarding these topics. If they do, they are liable to be litigated against.

During the interview be mindful of the questions that are being asked. If you're not considerable answering any questions or if you feel the interviewer has passed to a question that violates your rights, you can politely tell them that you do not feel comfortable answering this question and that they should not be asking you questions that do not pertain to the job responsibility.

Step 20

The Long Term Job Search

In the long term you will always need to keep your eyes open for the next career opportunity. In the Western world opportunities are abound and it's really important to align your life situation your career aspirations with what's available in the market. taking an inventory of your career every year is perhaps the best thing you can do for yourself and evaluate if your current job is providing you with what you need or if there are other opportunities that can help you grow financially mentally and career wise.

Something that'll keep you on top of things is to be aware of what is happening in your industry and in other companies such as the one that you are currently employed with. It's also good to be part of some kind of professional organizations, meet up groups and other industry associations and professional organizations. This will keep your mind fresh and also help engage with other people within the same or various industries.

I personally find that LinkedIn is a great option if you want to be aware of what's happening around you. Again on LinkedIn you are able to build a network, read news, join groups, and do so many other things that help you drive your career.

Step 21

Putting Everything Together

After landing in Canada, looking for a job is that probably the first thing you will do. Getting a great position where you can use your skills and help the organization grow and grow yourself as well is the best thing that can happen to you. After landing, stress levels are usually high just because you will begin the transition phase in your life. If you have a better planned job search strategy and you follow all the steps highlighted in this book you will definitely have an edge over other candidates you will also be able to source out job openings that relate well with your expectations. You will also be able to craft a great resume to use the insights and intelligence provided that will help enhance your job application.

I highly recommend that you use multiple sources to enhance all aspects of your job search. If you are looking for jobs on the internet, visit multiple websites and cross reference some of the trends in your particular industry. As you start cracking your resume refer to multiple books, websites and resources to make the best choices for your professional profile. Every resume is unique and you are unique as well so make sure that however you end up crafting your resume you make it the best it can be.

Local libraries in every Canadian community are a great resource when it comes to research and you will find hundreds of books in the career section of your neighborhood library. Use these resources that are available and do the best you can. Some community agency's provide help career counseling and guidance regarding and in some cases even placements. Use those resources to find a job for yourself and to enhance your career once you're in Canada.

I wish you all the best in your job search in Canada and hope that you're able to succeed and find the position that you strongly desire. I urge you to reach the peak of excellence during your job search. Stay focused and planned. This is very important as the job search process can take you in different paths, some of which can be very stressful. Learn how to make friends have to engage in communities and how to tap into the hidden job market by being proactive. This will deeply enhance your capabilities and reduce the time it takes you to look for a job, but more than anything else it will help you build a network of people and associates that you can count on.

Other Titles by the Author

Get Ahead

By Ian Khan

Hot Home business ideas for 2015. The book summarizes the type of business, main aspects, type of work. skills needed, investment needed and other informative data. Great for anyone who needs a quick reference on what business trends are hot in 2015. The 2015 classification has been done based on current business trends, small business success and other data.

Available on Amazon

Make me Like You

Get noticed, get hired. Learn how to get your resume to the top of the pile and then picked for an interview. Cut through the clutter and create a resume that delivers the home run. Get Top Tips to ensure while creating a resume that gets noticed. What does it take for such a resume to contain ? Learn this and more in Make Me Like You.

Available on Amazon

by IAN KHAN B.Eng, PMP, MCSE

Cloud Wars

The Cloud has come out of its early days and adoption to the Cloud is high. Solutions, platforms, Infrastructure and Services have all moved to the Cloud and as a result has everyone's attention. Today the Cloud industry is seeing unprecedented growth fuelled by cash rich companies who are willing to spend billions in technology development, acquisitions and simply getting ahead.

In Cloud Wars, learn about what is fuelling the growth, how consumer and enterprise demand is shaping the future and how the big boys in the software industry are rapidly waging war at each other to grab a bigger share of the pie.

Available on Amazon

"Simply Electrifying"

by IAN KHAN B.Eng, PMP, MCSE

How I Used an Easy Way to Stop Smoking Forever

How I Used an Easy Way to Stop Smoking Forever is a collection of insights from an ex-smoker into the psychology and challenges faced in quitting & how to overcome them. It is also a guide for smokers and people who want them to stop.

This book is not a manual of steps to stop smoking or techniques that will help you quit right away but more of a personal journey into how the author was able to stop smoking using powerful yet simple techniques that are in everyone's reach through their mind.

This book focuses on the mental game that is needed to succeed to create a life that is smoke free, healthy and has a much better quality of life.

Available on Amazon

Sell to Me

Get introduced to key business marketing lessons in the world of Enterprise Software Sales. Learn what drives revenues in the software sales world, marketing programs and creating unbeatable engagement with your prospects and customers.

Available on Amazon

The Enterprise Software Marketing Survival Guide

by IAN KHAN B.Eng, PMP, MCSE

Don't forget to Signup & receive insider benefits!

Join Ian's Readers VIP list today.

Signup at www.iankhan.com/newsletter